Royal Fireworks Language Arts by M

The Music of the Hemispheres

Poetics for Young Children

Second Edition

Michael Clay Thompson

Royal Fireworks Press
Unionville, New York

November 2021

Copyright © 2021 Royal Fireworks Online Learning, Inc.
Original publication copyright © 2004 Royal Fireworks Publishing Company, Inc.
All Rights Reserved. No copying, reproduction, or electronic dissemination
of this book is permitted without the express written consent of the publisher.

Royal Fireworks Press
41 First Avenue, P.O. Box 399
Unionville, NY 10988-0399
(845) 726-4444
fax: (845) 726-3824
email: mail@rfwp.com
website: rfwp.com

ISBN: 978-0-89824-672-8

Book design: Michael Clay Thompson
Publisher: Dr. T.M. Kemnitz
Editor: Jennifer Ault
Cover art: Milton N. Kemntiz
Cover designer: Kerri Ann Ruhl

Printed and bound in Unionville, New York, on acid-free paper
using vegetable-based inks at the Royal Fireworks facility. 10n21

local  363

For Myriam Borges Thompson

About the cover: The front cover is a painting by American artist Milton N. Kemnitz (1911-2005) of a part of the island he owned in McGregor Bay, in the north channel of Georgian Bay. Kemnitz spent part of each summer on that island between the late 1950s and the mid-1990s, and the art he created there is the basis of the illustrations in *Grammar Island* and *Sentence Island*, as well as for the covers of *Practice Island*.

Table of Contents

Preface

Poetry, real poetry, is an extraordinary art form.

Being a poet is much like being a composer of symphonies. Just as a composer writes each note on a musical staff, and composes harmonies for the different instruments, and knows when to enhance the percussion or the woodwinds, a great poet has an array of tools and techniques at hand and puts each sound on the page, one at a time, in a deliberately chosen rhythm, for a reason. A poet might spend a year carefully perfecting a fourteen-line sonnet.

This book, though it explores many powerful and technical things that poets can do with the sounds of words, is only a hint. It just cracks open the door, giving you a peek inside the huge world of creative life that poets live in.

Though this is but an introduction, it is nevertheless an introduction to the real thing. The purpose of this book is to find ways to reveal the reality of poem power, to give you an eyeball-to-the-letter closeup of what goes on in a poet's thought. The architect Mies van der Rohe said that God is in the details; I hope that by putting a microscope on the beautiful details of poetry, I can show how wonderful they are.

XXXIII

Emily Dickinson

How happy is the little stone
That rambles in the road alone,
And doesn't care about careers,
And exigencies never fears;
Whose coat of elemental brown
A passing universe put on;
And independent as the sun,
Associates or glows alone,
Fulfilling absolute decree
In casual simplicity.

The Music of the Hemispheres

In the medieval ages,
philosophers believed that each planet,
as it zoomed around in orbit,
made a sound...
a note.
The sound of all the planets in space
was called *the music of the spheres*.

Today, we say the human brain
has two hemispheres,
and through the magic of human language,
we have poetry,
the ***music of the hemispheres***.

Language is human.
Many animals make sounds,
but only human beings make language.

We love language for lots of reasons,
and one of the most important
is that we love the beautiful
sounds of language.

Words are made of sounds.

When we write words,
we show the sounds with letters.

The letter *s*
sounds like

SSSSSSSSSSSSSSSSSSS

Some sounds sound like
woodwinds,
or horns,
or wind in the trees.

whwh

eeee

u

Some sounds in words are like
sounds in nature:

This little piggy cried
Wee wee wee
all the way home.

This is called

onomatopoeia
(AH no MAH toe PEE uh).

plop
trickle
splash
ash
drip

There are two main kinds of sounds:
vowels and **consonants**.

Vowels sound like singing:

a e i o u y

and consonants sound like clicks, and taps, and bumps:

b c d f g h j k l m n p q r s t v w x z

We can even do a
vowel-consonant split
by putting vowels and consonants
on different lines.

What words are these?

```
  i  e
cr ck t

   o e
  fl w r

  u   e
 p ddl
```

By splitting the vowels away
from the consonants,
we can see and hear them more clearly.
We can even sing a word like a song!

baseball

a e a
b s b ll

b ay... ss b ahh... l...

Do you see that in the word *baseball*,
the first *a* and the second *a* have different sounds?

The first ***a*** in *baseball* sounds like ***ay***,
and the second ***a*** sounds like ***ah***.
There is even a third ***a*** sound, as in ***bat***.
And the ***e*** in *baseball* is silent!

So the vowels in *baseball*
sound like ***ay-ah***!

English has more sounds than letters,
so letters have to make several sounds
and also join with other letters to make
special combined sounds, like
sh, ***th***, ***ch***, and others.

The sounds of words almost
have personalities, like people.
The letter

m

is soft, like a hum,
and reassuring.
We find *m* in *mama*
and *Romeo*.

When the Scottish poet Robert Burns
wanted to communicate the
gentleness of love,
he filled his poem with *m*:

My Mary's asleep
by thy murmuring stream

There are lots of consonants
that are **soft**...

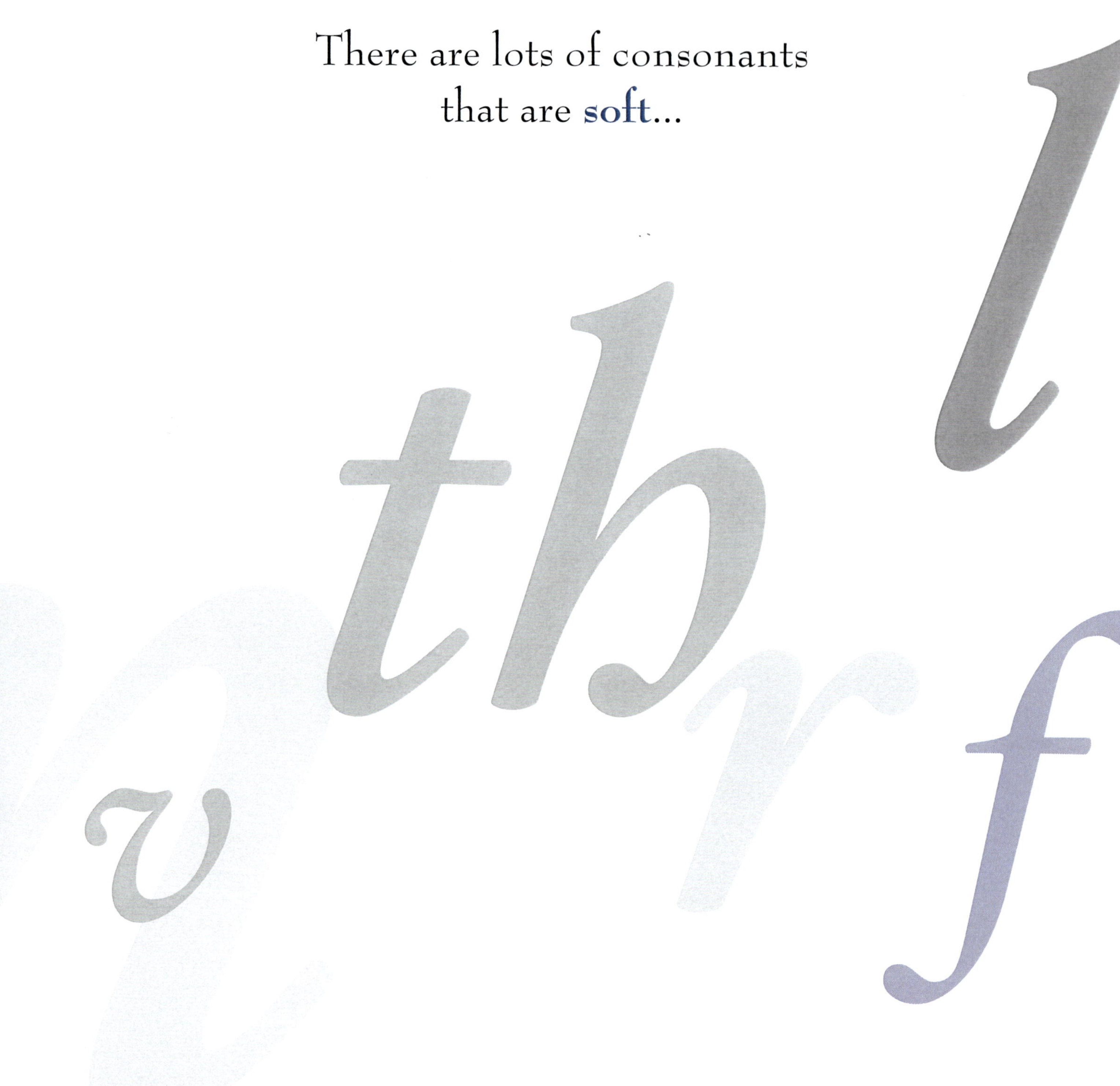

...and other consonants
that are **scratchy**, rough, or pounding.

Some consonants
are **hissy**, breathy, or windy.

w s h v w

In William Shakespeare's
love story *Romeo and Juliet*,
a play he wrote in poetry,
he wrote soft, beautiful sounds
for Juliet's lines.

Juliet asks Romeo
why he has to be named
Romeo. Their two families
are enemies, so Romeo
is the child of her father's foe:

O Romeo, Romeo,
Wherefore art thou
Romeo?
Deny thy father,
and refuse thy name.

(*Wherefore* means why.)

But in William Shakespeare's
witch story *Macbeth*,
also a play he wrote in poetry,
he wrote sharp, harsh, scratchy, evil sounds
for the witches to speak—
sounds like ***ake***, ***kaw***, and ***boi***:

Fillet of a fenny snake,
in the cauldron,
boil and bake.

Sometimes, poets hide
animal sounds
in their poetry,
and you hear them without
really realizing that you do.

In his tiny poem "Splinter,"
Carl Sandburg used the ***s*** sound to
represent a cricket's chirp,
and then he stopped, to let us feel the loss.
Do you hear the little cricket?
It stops, but then it returns and reassures us
with a pretty ***s*** and ***i*** song.

The voice of the last cricket,
Across the first frost,
Is one kind of good-bye.
It is so thin a splinter of singing.

SS SS SS SS SS SS SS SS

In his poem "The Cloud,"
the English poet Percy Bysshe Shelley
used drenched, rainy sounds,
such as ***rs***, and ***sh***, and ***fr***,
to capture the sound
of rain.

Shelley imagined the cloud
as if it were a person.
"I bring...," says the cloud.
Portraying an object as a person
is called *personification*.

I bring fresh showers
for the thirsting flowers
From the seas
and the streams.

You begin to notice
that lots of words,
such as ***drip***, ***drop***, ***splash***, and ***trickle***,
sound just like
what they stand for.

The word *drip*
sounds like a drip.

drip!

drip

splash

drop drop

drop

splash

drip

drop

drop

drop

drip

drop

drop

rip

drop drop

drip

drip

drip

splash

drip

splash

onomatopoeia

The word *whistle*
sounds like a whistle,
with its *wh* and *s* sounds.

Robert Burns used *whistle*
to evoke the sounds of the blackbirds
in his poem "Afton Water."

wh

Thou stock dove whose echo
resounds thro the glen,
Ye wild **whistling** blackbirds
in yon thorny den,
Thou green-crested lapwing,
thy screaming forbear—
I charge you,
disturb not my slumbering fair!

Another kind of sound,
different from vowels and consonants,
is the *stress*.

When we speak,
we say some parts of words
with more emphasis,
more firmness,
more volume.
We stress certain parts of words.

*mon*key

When we say the word *monkey*,
the first syllable is stressed.

We say MONkey,
not monKEY, and
TIger, not tiGER.

What is a *syllable*?
It is a part of a word that we speak
with a single effort of our voice.
In the word *feather*,
feath is a syllable,
and *er* is a syllable.

In the word *petunia*,
we speak three syllables.
They sound like
peh toon yuh.

feathe

Look at these syllables:

pudding	marigold
pud ding	**mar** i gold
subtraction	poet
sub **trac** tion	**po** et
Jennifer	Argentina
Jen ni fer	Ar gen **ti** na

pe**tun**ia

Because some syllables
are stressed, and others are not,
we can create patterns of stresses,
and this can make
a wavy sound,
a rhythm
like a heartbeat.

Look at these lines from
Shakespeare's Sonnet 73,
with the stressed syllables darkened:

That time of year thou mayst in me behold
When yellow leaves, or none, or few, do hang
Upon those boughs which shake against the cold,
Bare ruined choirs where late the sweet birds sang.

In the first three lines,
every second syllable is stressed.
It makes a nice, regular wave.
Shakespeare's first three lines each have ten syllables.
How is the fourth line different?

Beginning with a stressed syllable, Shakespeare's fourth line is clearly different from the first three that are written in perfect iambic pentameter. Although the word *ruined* sometimes sounds like a two-syllable word, as when someone wails, "I am ruined!" the context of this line is an emphatic PULSE: *cold, bare, ruined choirs*, that then shifts into three perfect iambs for the birdsong. If we read *ruined* as a two-syllable word, with the second syllable unstressed, then that brings attention to the idea of being ruined. Poets often use a single out-of-pattern foot to call attention to a word. If we read *ruined* as one syllable, with the second half of the word absorbed into the first half, then the line has only nine syllables—not an unusual technique. If we read *ruined* as two syllables, then the line has the ten syllables of the first three lines. This opens up a wonderful discussion.

If we look at this line from Robert Burns
once more and darken the stressed syllables,
it looks like this:

My ***Ma*** *ry's a* ***sleep***
by thy ***mur*** *mur ing* ***stream***

Robert Burns put two unstressed
syllables between each of the stressed syllables.
Why would he do that
in a description of a stream?
Do you think a stream has a perfectly regular beat?

m

m

m

My Mary's asleep
by thy murmuring stream,
flow gently, sweet Afton,
disturb not her dream.

Let's have some fun!

Think of something that makes sounds.
Anything.
Baby chickens.
The wind in the palm trees.
The pot boiling on the stove.
Laughter at the playground.
Your dog barking at a squirrel.
Anything.

Then, write about it, but fiddle with the words until you get **words that sound like the subject**. If it is baby chickens, you need *peep peep* sounds, so you might use words like *keep*, *sleep*, *steep*, or *jeep*. If it is your dog, you might use growly words like *grump*, *grouch*, *rough*, and *gotcha*!

The Owl in the Moonwind

Michael Clay Thompson

A hidden "Whoo?" in silver night,
Black branches crossed the moon.
"Who's there," I cried, but silence—soon
A hidden voice replied.
"Who? and Who? and Who?" it called.
"It's me, sir," I said, small.
But no response came from the tree.
Dark wind began to fall;
It whirled around the midnight wood.
The leaves were rustling; all
My hair stood right on end; I couldn't
Move.

Are you beginning to think
that poets are aware
of every sound in their poems,
just as composers know
each note in their compositions?

You are right.
Poets know all the vowel sounds,
and all the consonant sounds,
and all the stresses,
and they arrange these sounds
at the same time that they arrange
the meanings of words.

1 Rhyme *time*

Poets often put **rhymes** in poems.

A rhyme is a similar sound found
in two different words,
such as *rhyme* and *time*,
monarchy and *malarkey*.

The sounds do not
have to be spelled alike.

The team

had a scheme

it would seem!

If the lines
rhyme at their ends,
that is called

end rhyme.

end

Weary with toil, I haste me to my bed, a
The dear repose for limbs with travel tired, b
But then begins a journey in my head a
To work my mind when body's work's expired. b

from Sonnet 27
William Shakespeare

Rhyme Scheme

If we want to study the **rhyme scheme** of a poem, we assign the letter *a* to the first rhyme sound, and the letter *b* to the second rhyme sound, and so on. So the **rhyme scheme** of this poem is *abab*. The **a** rhymes are **bed** and **head**, and the **b** rhymes are **tired** and **expired**.

Emily Dickinson
used end rhyme
in this poem about a flower,
the gentian.
Dickinson rhymed the even lines,
2, 4, 6, and 8,
but not the odd ones.

God made a little gentian: a
It tried to be a rose b
And failed, and all the summer laughed. c
But just before the snows b
There came a purple creature d
That ravished all the hill; e
And summer hid her forehead, f
And mockery was still. e

from XLVII
Emily Dickinson

Rhymes put
inside the lines are called

internal rhyme.

Shakespeare used internal rhyme in:

Double, **double**, toil and **trouble**.

William Blake
used both end rhyme
and internal rhyme
in his poem "The Tiger."

In what distant deeps or **skies** a
Burnt the **fire** of thine **eyes**! a
On what wings dare he **aspire**? b
What the hand, dare seize the **fire**? b

from "The Tiger"
William Blake

The British novelist and poet
Thomas Hardy used subtle internal near rhyme
in these lines from his 1900 poem
"The Darkling Thrush"
about a little bird that sings
his heart out, even in a bleak landscape.
Darkling means in the dark.

An aged **thrush**, frail, gaunt, and small, a
In blast-beruffled plume, b
Had chosen **thus** to fling his soul c
Upon the growing gloom. b

from "The Darkling Thrush"
Thomas Hardy

If a poet makes a rhyme
out of two words that look alike
but do not sound alike
(Goosey, goosey **gander**, whither shall I **wander**),
this is called

eye rhyme.

Though and *tough* are eye rhyme.
Ralph Waldo Emerson
used eye rhyme in his poem "Brahma."
The adjective *slain* and the adverb *again*
both end in *-ain*, but they do not sound the same.
They rhyme to the eye, not to the ear.
Emerson used eye rhyme to make an end rhyme!

If the red slayer think he slays,
Or if the slain think he is **slain**,
They know not well the subtle ways
I keep, and pass, and turn **again**.

from "Brahma"
Ralph Waldo Emerson

Let's have some rhyme fun!

On a clean sheet of paper,
write groups of words that rhyme.
In one place, you might write words
like *feet*, *neat*, *sheet*, and *sleet*.
In another place, you might write words
like *mash*, *crash*, *flash*, and even *attach*!

Once you have piles of rhymes
to think about, write a poem
that has as many rhymes as possible,
including end rhymes, internal rhymes,
and even eye rhymes!

The Puddle and the Chicken

Michael Clay Thompson

A stricken chicken staggered forth
and tried to cross the road;
it wobbled left and toppled right,
and hopped, and flopped, and strode.
But dead ahead a puddle was,
and chickens don't like mud.

The chicken ducked and clucked because
the puddle wasn't subtle;
it reeked of muck, and then a truck
came, splashing, on the double!
With squawks and gobbles, suddenly
the chicken wobbled free,
but walls of yuck came from the truck
and splashed him with debris.

The chicken had to cough,
enough.

Allite

Rhyme is not all that poets use
to compose the sounds of poems.
Another technique is alliteration,
the repetition of the first, *initial*, sounds of words:
"Baa, baa, black sheep."
Alliteration lets us emphasize a sound
that is perfect for the meaning.
Robert Burns used alliteration:

ration

John Anderson my jo, John,
When we were first aquent:
Your locks were like the raven,
Your **b**ony **b**row was **b**rent.

from "John Anderson, My Jo"
Robert Burns

(The word *brent* means smooth in Scottish.)

William Shakespeare
used **alliteration** on the letter ***s*** in Sonnet 30.
Notice the interesting eye rhyme
with *past* and *waste*.

When to the **s**essions of **s**weet **s**ilent thought
I **s**ummon up remembrance of things **past**,
I **s**igh the lack of many a thing I **s**ought,
and with old woes new wail my dear Time's **waste**.

Alliteration often takes the form
of an adjective and its noun
that begin with the same letter.
A.E. Housman used alliteration this way
in "To an Athlete Dying Young":

So set, before its echoes fade,
the fleet foot on the sill of shade,
And hold to the low lintel up
The still-defended challenge cup.

adj. n.
fleet foot

One poem may have
end rhyme, internal rhyme,
eye rhyme and alliteration, and more.
Look at these lines from
William Butler Yeats's (pronounced Yates) poem
"The Lake Isle of Innisfree."
Innisfree is a lake in County Sligo, Ireland.

I will arise and go now, for always night and **day**
I hear **l**ake water **l**apping with **l**ow sounds by the **shore**:
While I stand on the **road****way**, or on the pavements **gray**,
I hear it in the deep heart's **core**.

Notice how Yeats supports the alliterated *l*'s
with lots of other *l*'s inside words in this passage.

I hear lake water
lapping
with low sounds
by the shore.

Here are some lines from
William Shakespeare's play
The Taming of the Shrew.
In the play, these lines are spoken
by the gruff Petruchio to his wife, Katherine.
Just look at how much poetry
Shakespeare poured into Petruchio's speech:

And now, my honey love,
Will **w**e return unto thy **f**ather's house
And revel it as **b**ravely as the **b**est,
With silken **c**oats and **c**aps and golden **rings**,
With **ruffs** and **cuffs** and **f**arthingales and **things**:
With scarfs and **f**ans and double change of **brav'ry**,
With amber **b**racelets, **b**eads, and all this **knav'ry**.

from *The Taming of the Shrew*, IV. iii., Petruchio
William Shakespeare

In Petruchio's gorgeous words, we see end rhyme,
internal rhyme, and lots of alliteration.
But there is even more poetry
hidden in the passage. Look at the play
of sound in words like *revel* and *bravely*,
farthingales and *scarfs*, *coats* and *golden*,
amber and *bracelets* and *brav'ry*.

Not only that, look how most of the lines have
exactly ten syllables, with every second syllable stressed:

1 2 3 4 5 6 7 8 9 10
With ruffs and cuffs and farthingales and things

If we darken the stressed syllables, it looks like:

And **now**, my **hon**ey **love**,
Will **we** re**turn** un**to** thy **fa**ther's **house**
And **re**vel **it** as **bra**vely **as** the **best**,
With **sil**ken **coats** and **caps** and **gol**den **rings**,
With **ruffs** and **cuffs** and **far**thin**gales** and **things**:
With **scarfs** and **fans** and **doub**le **change** of **bra**v'ry,
With **am**ber **bra**celets, **beads**, and **all** this **kna**v'ry.

from *The Taming of the Shrew*, IV. iii., Petruchio
William Shakespeare

Beyond rhyme and alliteration,
poets create hidden echoes and threads
of sound that are only visible
if you look very closely.

far

scarfs

coats and

golden

ingales

bravely
revel

bracelets

If we look at the **consonants** in Petruchio's words, we see that Shakespeare has loaded the lines with soft, rich sounds: ***w***'s, ***r***'s, ***f***'s, ***v***'s, ***l***'s, ***th***'s. The passage drips with richness and luxury, with sounds that enhance the images of fine clothing and jewelry.

And now, my honey love,
Will we return unto thy father's house
And revel it as bravely as the best,
With silken coats and caps and golden rings,
With ruffs and cuffs and farthingales and things:
With scarfs and fans and double change of brav'ry,
With amber bracelets, beads, and all this knav'ry.

from *The Taming of the Shrew*, IV. iii., Petruchio
William Shakespeare

Let's have some sound fun!

Think of a situation
in which one sound would be important.
If the kettle were steaming,
the important sound might be *ssssss*.
If you were hammering nails,
the important sounds might be *b d b d b*.
When you have your situation and your sound,
then write a poem that contains
as much of that sound as possible.
If you want to emphasize two sounds,
that is all right.

The Blue Reef

Michael Clay Thompson

Shoals of blue fish swirled and bloomed,
and bubbles rose in lines above the coral;
floral blades of seaweed curled and waved,
and blank-eyed blackfish swished in shadows
where the blowfish wished the blue crabs bluffed.
Above the blundering waves the blinding sun
began its burn across the sky; the blue wind blew enough;
the rough surf crashed into the reef; it boomed,
and from the deep, the blue whale
crooned its long tune.

The Adventure of Language History

In poetry, meter is the pattern of stressed and unstressed syllables in the lines of the poem. The English word *meter* comes from the ancient Greek word *metron*, which in Greek letters looked like μετρον. It is fun to see the Greek letters and to get a feeling for the ancient origins of English. The Romans were influenced by the Greeks and brought many Greek words into Latin.

The brain is wider than the sky...
Emily Dickinson

3

μετρον
meter

Just as songs have rhythm,
traditional English poems have
rhythm, which is part of what
makes them beautiful or in some
cases just effective.

The word *rhythm* comes
from the ancient Greek ρνθμοσ,
pronounced *rhythmos*,
which meant measure.

The rhythm of a poem,
the pattern of repetition, the beat,
is called the ***meter***.

Each unit of meter is called a *foot*.
There are different types of poetic foot.
In an **iambic foot**, there are two syllables,
and the second syllable is stressed:
The **ants** go **march**ing **one** by **one**, hur**rah**, hur**rah**!
A line may have one or more iambs in it,
though most lines have three to five.
Emily Dickinson alternated
four-iamb lines and three-iamb lines
in her poem CXXVI:

The **brain** is **wi**der **than** the **sky**,
For, **put** them **side** by **side**,
The **one** the **oth**er **will** in**clude**
With **ease**, and **you** be**side**.

Let's look more closely.
In line one, the first iamb is *The brain*.
The first syllable is *The*, and it is not stressed.
The second syllable is *brain*, and it is stressed.
That makes one iamb: a two-syllable foot,
with the stress on the second syllable.
The next iamb is made of a whole word, *is*,
and the first syllable of the next word, *wi*.
So the first two iambs are:
The brain / is wi...
Can you hear the iambic meter?
da DA, da DA, da DA, da DA

If we use **slashes** to separate the iambs, we see:

The

The brain / is wi /der than / the sky,
For, put / them side / by side,
The one / the oth / er will / include
With ease, / and you / beside.

brain / is wi

There are four main types of poetic foot
(iambs, trochees, dactyls, and anapests),
but the iambic foot is the most common.
It imitates the natural beat
of English conversation, right?

William Wordsworth used **four iambs per line**
for his poem "I Wandered Lonely as a Cloud":

I **wan**dered **lone**ly **as** a **cloud**
That **floats** on **high** o'er **vales** and **hills**,
When **all** at **once** I **saw** a **crowd**,
A **host**, of **gol**den **daffo**dils.

I wan / dered lon /ely as / a cloud
That floats / on high / o'er vales, / and hills,
When all / at once / I saw / a crowd,
A host, / of gol / den daf / fo dils.

In ancient Greek,
tri meant three,
tetra meant four,
and *penta* meant five.
We still retain these stems in English words today.
A line of three iambs is **iambic trimeter**.
A line of four iambs is **iambic tetrameter**.
And a line of five iambs is **iambic pentameter**.

3 trimeter
4 tetrameter
5 pentameter

ama

William Shakespeare used iambic pentameter
extensively in his plays.
Here is a line of iambic pentameter
from Shakespeare's comedy
A Midsummer Night's Dream:

My lord, I shall reply amazedly.
My **lord** / I **shall** / re**ply** / a**maz** / ed**ly**.

Notice that the one word *amazedly*
has four syllables that make two iambs.
Two iambs in one word!

zedly

Now, let us look at part of
John Keats's (pronounced Keets) poem
"On First Looking into Chapman's Homer."
In this poem you can find
iambic pentameter,
end rhyme, eye rhyme, and alliteration:

Much have I traveled in the realms of **gold,**
And many goodly states and kingdoms **seen;**
Round many western islands have I **been**
Which bards in fealty to Apollo **hold.**
Oft of **one wide** expanse had I been **told...**

Do you see the eye rhyme of *seen* and *been*?
The end rhyme of *gold, seen, been, hold,* and *told*?
The very subtle alliteration of *one wide*?
One and *wide* do not begin with the same letter;
they begin with the same sound!
Do you hear the iambic pentameter?
And **ma** / ny **good** / ly **states** / and **king** / doms **seen**.
(Some of the lines are not exact iambic pentameter.)

Poets control the things
we have learned—and more.
It sometimes took
the poet Dylan Thomas more than
a year to write one **sonnet**
(a fourteen-line poem of iambic tetrameter).
In the poem on the next page,
can you find iambic tetrameter, iambic pentameter,
end rhyme, eye rhyme, internal rhyme,
onomatopoeia, and alliteration?
What is the rhyme scheme?

A wild wind rose and waved the bough,
with whooo and whihhh and shhhh, but how
the bending branches bent we did not know....
We smiled; not knowing was enough.

Three more types of poetic foot?

As we mentioned, even though the **iamb**
is the most common foot in English poetry,
there are three other main types of foot.

The first is the **trochee**.
A trochee is a backwards iamb:
a two-syllable foot with the stress on the first syllable.

double, **fen**ny, **caul**dron

or

Eencey, **ween**cey **spi**der...

Since English is naturally iambic,
iambic lines sound happy,
normal, reassuring.

Poets use trochaic lines to create the opposite effect.
If they want to create a feeling of danger or evil,
they use **trochees, the iamb-cancelers**!
Shakespeare used trochaic tetrameter
for the witches' chant in *Macbeth*:

Double double, toil and trouble

1 2 3 4
Doub le / **doub** le / **toil** and / **troub** le

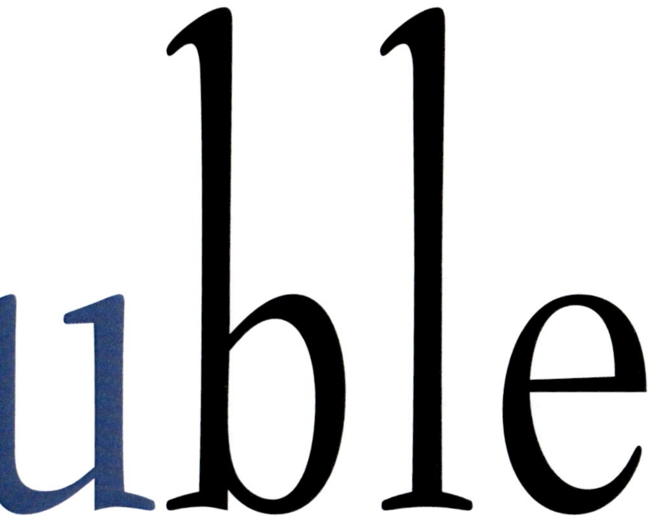

William Blake used **trochaic tetrameter**
to suggest danger in his poem "The Tiger,"
but he added a trick:
he dropped the unstressed syllable
from the fourth trochee
and let the line end with force.
So instead of

DA da DA da DA da DA da,

it sounds like

DA da DA da DA da DAH!

And then he switched
to iambic tetrameter in the fourth line!

Tiger, **Ti**ger, **bur**ning **bright** a
In the **for**ests **of** the **night**; a
What im**mor**tal **hand** or **eye**, b
Could **frame** thy **fear**ful **sym**me**try**? b

Notice the alliteration:
burning bright,
forests, frame, fearful.

The iamb is a two-syllable foot, and so is the trochee.
The other two types of foot have **three** syllables.
We are not going to emphasize these now, but
just so you will have heard of them, their names are:

anapest

a three-syllable foot with the third syllable stressed:

and the **dish** ran a**way** with the **spoon**!

Dylan Thomas used anapestic trimeter:

...though I **sang** in my **chains** like the **sea**

dactyl

a three-syllable foot with the first syllable stressed:
"**Hig**glety, **pig**glety..."
Alfred, Lord Tennyson,
used dactyls to sound like hoofbeats
in his poem "Charge of the Light Brigade."

Half a league, **half** a league,
Half a league **on**ward,
All in the **val**ley of **Death**
Rode the six **hun**dred.
"**For**ward, the **Light** Brigade!
Charge for the **guns**!" he said:
Into the **val**ley of **Death**
Rode the six **hun**dred.

Meter

foot: the repeating rhythm in a line of poetry

iamb: two-syllable foot, stress on second (- /)
trochee: two-syllable foot, stress on first (/ -)
anapest: three-syllable foot, stress on third (- - /)
dactyl: three-syllable foot, stress on first (/ - -)

monometer: a one-foot line
dimeter: a two-foot line
trimeter: a three-foot line
tetrameter: a four-foot line
pentameter: a five-foot line

A poem in iambic pentameter:

The ridges of the shell are ivory waves
That cover up a squishy guy inside;
He peeks out slowly right and left and saves
Himself by closing up the shell to hide!

Let's have some foot fun!

Think about the four different
types of poetic foot.
Each foot makes its own rhythm,
and these rhythms remind us of sounds we know.
Dactyls may remind us of horses,
and iambs of heartbeats.
Trochees may remind us of hammers pounding,
and anapests of streams flowing.
The **rise** and **fall** of **syllables**
in **dai**ly **Eng**lish **tends** to **be** i**am**bic, **right**?
So pick a foot, then pick a meter, and write a poem!
Here is one in trochaic tetrameter:

Battle Dwarves

Michael Clay Thompson

Down the mountain dwarves came tramping,
Dusty clouds and dirty stamping,
Down the tunnels, 'round the pounding
Waterfalls all splashy sounding.
"Hi de ho!" the dwarves sang gayly.
"Ho de hi!" they chanted daily.
Down the paths great warrior columns,
Marching toward the greeny gollums,
Blang! and Bling! their battle axes,
Banged stones practicing attacks as
Waiting for them gollums gathered
Far below in ambush as their
Enemy approached the path heard
tramp, tramp, tramp!

Let's put things together.

Let's try to combine
some of the elements of poetry
that we have learned.
We could use end rhyme,
internal rhyme, and eye rhyme.
We could use alliteration and onomatopoeia.
We could use two different types
of foot in the same poem.
We could even vary the meter.
This may take a lot of thinking....
If we used four lines of iambic tetrameter
and four lines of anapestic tetrameter....

Sun, Moon, Earth, Squirrel

Michael Clay Thompson

Fire flared from the solar surface;
its yellow light streaked into space.
Eight minutes it blazed,
ninety-three million miles,
struck the Moon's gray circled-cratered plain,
and glanced away again, blue and unphased.

The sunlight, now moonlight,
bounced toward midnight Earth—
239,000 miles in one-point-three seconds—
blue spears of moon-bounced
sun-moon-light falling here,
down the silent owl-hoo atmosphere,
down upon the dark wild wood.

Curled in his leaf-house the sleeping squirrel
slept on, dreamed of green tree-days,
as landing light fell upon his fur and faded,
leaving him still a-nap in squirrel dreams,
running out on dream branches, leaping,
his fur softly lit by blue moonlight
from the yellow sun.

one

Baa, baa, black sheep,
Have you any wool?
Yes, sir, yes, sir,
Three bags full.

two

One for my master,
One for my dame,
And one for the little boy
Who lives down the lane.

three

Baa, baa, black sheep,
Have you any wool?
Yes, sir, yes, sir,
Three bags full.

4 stanza

Poems often have sections called **stanzas**. A twenty-line poem might be divided into five four-line stanzas. For example, a four-line stanza is called a ***quatrain***.

STANZA

A stanza is a section of a poem,
like a room is a part of a house.
In many poems, the stanza
is based on the form.

For example, an **English sonnet**
is a fourteen-line poem made of four stanzas:
three **quatrains** (four-line stanzas)
and a **couplet** (a two-line stanza).
All of the lines of the sonnet are iambic pentameter.
The sonnet rhyme scheme is *abab cdcd efef gg*.

Let's look at Shakespeare's Sonnet 73 again:

sonnet: three quatrai

That time of year thou mayst in me behold a
When yellow leaves, or none, or few, do hang b
Upon those boughs which shake against the cold, a
Bare ruined choirs, where late the sweet birds sang. b

In me thou see'st the twilight of such day c
As after sunset fadeth in the west; d
Which by and by black night doth take away, c
Death's second self, that seals up all in rest. d

In me thou see'st the glowing of such fire, e
that on the ashes of his youth doth lie, f
As the deathbed whereon it must expire, e
Consumed with that which it was nourished by. f

This thou perceiv'st, which makes thy love more strong, g
To love that well which thou must leave ere long. g

s and a couplet

What do we learn from looking at a sonnet like this?
Well, this is a very advanced poem; in fact,
it is one of the best poems ever written,
and it would be a challenge to understand
each line and idea in the poem.
But what it does show us, even from the beginning,
is that poetry is a real
intellectual accomplishment.
To do all of the things that make great poetry
requires talent and knowledge.
Poetry is special.
Every stress, every vowel and consonant sound,
every stanza, every rhyme scheme—
the poet arranges all of it.
Here are a few of the things to notice:

iambic pentameter
(all 14 lines)

k sound
for the shaking
branches

s's for
birdsongs

Sonnet 73
William Shakespeare

three
quatrains

end rhyme

That **time of year** thou mayst in me behold
When yellow leaves, or none, or few, do hang
Upon those boughs which shake against the cold,
Bare ruined choirs, where late the sweet birds sang.

In me thou see'st **the twilight** of such day
As after sunset fadeth in the west;
Which by and by black night doth take away,
Death's second self, that seals up all in rest.

alliteration

In me thou see'st **the glowing** of such fire,
that on the ashes of his youth doth lie,
As the deathbed whereon it must expire,
Consumed with that which it was nourished by.

Notice *th* sounds:

couplet

This thou perceiv'st, which makes thy love more strong,
To love that well which thou must leave ere long.

alliteration

A series of poetic
comparisons called
metaphors; we'll learn
about them next.

So, what are some common
stanza forms in English poetry?
There are lots and lots. And lots.
But here are a few.
The **couplet** is a two-line stanza.
The **triplet** is a three-line stanza.
A **quatrain** is a four-line stanza.
A **quintet** is a five-line stanza.

lu

Let's look at one more: the ballad stanza.

A **ballad stanza** is four lines, *abcb*,
in which lines one and three are iambic tetrameter,
and lines two and four are iambic trimeter.
Remember Emily Dickinson's poem
about the brain? It was a ballad!

Robert Burns (1759-1796) and Sir Walter Scott created Scottish literature; before them, no one wrote literature in the Scottish dialect. Here are two stanzas from Burns's ballad "A Red Red Rose":

As fair art thou, my bonnie lass,
So deep in luve am I;
And I will luve thee still, my dear,
Till a' the seas gang dry.

Till a' the seas gang dry, my dear,
And the rocks melt wi' the sun;
I will luve thee still, my dear,
While the sands o' life shall run.

Let's look more closely.

Here is one stanza from Burns's ballad,
which contained four ballad stanzas in all.

Lines one and three are iambic tetrameter.
Lines two and four are iambic trimeter.
Lines two and four rhyme; one and three do not;
the end rhyme is *I* and *dry*.

Love is spelled *luve*, the Scottish way.

It is a perfect ballad stanza.

As **fair** art **thou**, my **bon**nie **lass**, a
So **deep** in **luve** am **I**; b
And **I** will **luve** thee **still**, my **dear**, c
Till **a'** the **seas** gang **dry**. b

Would you like to see the whole poem,
with all four ballad stanzas?

A Red, Red Rose

O my Luve's like a red, red rose,
That's newly sprung in June:
O my Luve's like the melodie
That's sweetly played in tune.

As fair art thou, my bonnie lass,
So deep in luve am I;
And I will luve thee still, my dear,
Till a' the seas gang dry.

Till a' the seas gang dry, my dear,
And the rocks melt wi' the sun;
I will luve thee still, my dear,
While the sands o' life shall run.

And fare thee weel, my only Luve,
And fare thee weel a while!
And I will come again, my Luve,
Though it were ten thousand mile.

When Robert Burns died in 1796, 10,000 people walked or rode on horseback to get to his funeral.

5

personification

similes

metaphors

figures of speech

Poets decide how their poems will sound,
but how? Why would a poet choose
one type of sound over another?

This is where **meaning** comes in.
The sound is a reflection
of what the poem is about.
It is a type of soundtrack for the idea.

Shakespeare used soft sounds for Juliet's
words to reveal the gentleness of her spirit.
Yeats used dozens of *l*'s in his poem
about the Lake of Innisfree to capture the sound
of lake water lapping on the shore.

fi

Are there other techniques poets can use to express their meanings in powerful ways?

Perhaps the two most famous techniques are the **simile** and the **metaphor**. They are called ***figures of speech***. A figure of speech is an indirect way of explaining one thing by comparing it to something else.

When Robert Burns said that "my Luve's like a red, red rose," that was a **simile**, pronounced SIM ih lee.

SIMILE

A **simile** is an openly expressed comparison that uses words such as *like* or *as*.

Robert Burns used a simile, as we have seen:

O my Luve's like a red, red rose.

The British poet George Gordon, Lord Byron, used a simile when he wrote that:

The Assyrian came down like a wolf on the fold.

Emily Dickinson used a simile
in this brilliant line:

The thought is quiet as a flake,—

By saying that a thought is as quiet AS a flake,
she constructed a simile.

But...how is a thought like a flake?
Similes (and metaphors, as we will see)
can be great ideas!

In 350 B.C.E. the ancient Greek philosopher Aristotle, who was the personal teacher of Alexander the Great, wrote a book about poetry called *The Poetics*. Aristotle gave examples of similes:

"We may say that a flute-player is *like* a monkey....
It is possible to say that...a ruin is *like* a house in rags....
Those legs of his curl just *like* parsley leaves...."

metap

METAPHOR

"The hills are like waves" is a simile, but
"The hills are waves" is a metaphor.
Metaphors do not use *like* or *as*.
Metaphors often use IS or ARE.

In a metaphor we compare two things
by saying they are the same thing:

Feelings **are** feathers in the wind.

Aristotle said that metaphors should be made
"from things that are related to the original thing,
and yet not obviously so related—
just as in philosophy also
an acute mind will perceive resemblances
even in things far apart."

One kind of metaphor is *personification*, in which we describe an object as though it were a person, as Shelley did in "The Cloud."

Sometimes the resemblance in a metaphor is very far apart.
In Shakespeare's play *Macbeth*,
Macbeth turns to Lady Macbeth and cries out, trying to express the torment of guilt he is feeling:

"Full of scorpions is my mind, dear wife!"

Macbeth does not have to say *like* or *as*.
We know Macbeth does not mean that his head is filled with real scorpions.
It is only a figure of speech. Just a metaphor.
But what a metaphor!

In Shakespeare's play *Romeo and Juliet*,
Romeo explains to Juliet how he climbed the stone walls that surrounded her orchard to find her:

With love's light wings did I o'erperch these walls,
For stony limits cannot hold love out,
And what love can do, that dares love attempt.

Romeo did not really use wings to fly over the walls; it is a metaphor. And when Juliet's nurse wants to praise the young Count Paris, she uses a metaphor to compare him to a perfect man, a wax model:

A man, young lady, such a man
As all the world—why, he's a man of wax.

In 1914 young British poet Rupert Brooke,
who had gone to France in World War I, wrote:

If I should die, think only this of me,
That there's some **corner** of a foreign field
That **is forever England.**

In saying that this corner IS England,
Brooke was constructing a metaphor.
The piece of ground (his grave) is not really England,
but by saying so, Brooke gave a beautiful
statement of love of his native land.

There's some corner of a foreign field
That is forever England.
– Rupert Brooke

Look carefully at the poem
on the following page.
Can you find all of these things?

iambic pentameter
iambic tetrameter
trochaic tetrameter
end rhyme
eye rhyme
internal rhyme
alliteration
quatrain
couplet
ballad stanza
metaphor
simile

The Ocean

Michael Clay Thompson

The long waves rolled toward the shore,
and cold foam shook the aging pier.
The rising walls of gray approached—a roar—
a crash, and rumbling clouds were tumbling near.

Above a soaring seagull cried, and turned,
flew past, head down, descending down the wind,
his eye-dot fixed us for a second, learned
our eyes, discerned us in his seagull mind.

The ocean is a moving plain,
with flowers made of foam;
the ocean's like a sea-god's rib,
slow-breathing, and alone.

Down the seagull drops and never
blinks until he hits the water.

Let's have some fun!

You know that a **metaphor**
is a comparison,
in which we learn about something
by seeing that it is like something else.
The key is to be original
and to pick something very far apart
from the target so that it is surprising,
as if we said that
"**Loyalty is a lunar orbit**."
Let us write a poem
based on a metaphor.
Use a lot of detail and imagination.
This model also uses *personification*:

Dawn

Michael Clay Thompson

Night, that shady coward, was slinking down the mountain.
He always ran from her.
In the field by the forest, she saw the people waking,
black spots in the gray chill,
their fires orange sparks against the hill.
She heard the clinky clatter of pans and spears,
the horses' voices hooeying.
She'd give 'em a show this morning.
She crept close, looked down at her fingers;
they began their slow glow—red, redder—
crouching behind the hill she stuck her left hand up
above the trees, and wooooo, the beams leaped up the sky,
and then the right hand, high—and held them out together,
wiggling fingers, streaming beams, and wow,
now they'd know that she was here, all right.
She held both hands out, fingers wide,
and gleamed away the night.

Poems are
imaginary gardens,
with real toads in them.

-Marianne Moore

POEMS

Marianne Moore said that poems are imaginary gardens with real toads in them. Real toads, however, don't come easy. What we have learned is that poets are special writers who know how to push language to its limits in order to say true things. Like composers of music, these composers of words do everything possible to create the most extraordinary expressions and observations. Poets are not just language decorators, trying to arrange pretty words; they are more like scientists or detectives, who give their lives to discover what is unknown and then try to make a true report.

Even in our brief introduction to poetry, we have seen that poets can play language like an instrument, rhyming words at the ends of lines or within the lines, giving the lines a regular rhythm by arranging words based on the stresses of their syllables, and setting up groups of words that all begin with a sound that is important to the idea of the poem. Poets can emphasize certain vowels, certain consonants, and can make poems sound like animals or events in the world. Poets can cast light on something by comparing it to something else in wonderful ways. All of these things take thought.

The poet Dylan Thomas would write long letters, discussing a few words he was considering for a poem. Working alone, he would read his poems aloud, in a loud voice, so that he could really hear the small surfaces of sound in the words. If Thomas was writing a sonnet, he would use fourteen separate pages, leaving himself an entire page for the revisions of each line. Only when he had all the problems worked out would he combine the fourteen lines together on a single page.

Poetry is an art, and poets are artists. Just as great painters might do dozens of pencil sketches and watercolors in order to work out the details of a painting they are planning, poets might work for a long time to find the details of sound, meaning, and originality that make a poem.

A word is dead
When it is said,
Some say.
I say it just
Begins to live
That day.

– Emily Dickinson

Greece and Rome

It is interesting that even though most of the advanced vocabulary words in English come from the Latin of the Romans, when we begin to study English poetry, we discover that many words about poetry come not from the Romans but from the ancient Greeks.

The rise of Greek culture preceded the rise of the Roman Empire, and the Romans were powerfully influenced by the Greeks. They admired their architecture, their art, and their poetry. The Romans borrowed Greek words and hired Greek artists. When you look up English words in a good dictionary, you will notice that many words come from Latin, but they show Greek origins prior to that. The Romans had borrowed them!

The Romans brought organization, military might, law, authority, and concrete to the world; the Greeks brought philosophy, poetry, mythology, and Greek temples, with their beautiful columns.

In order to understand ourselves, we must notice those parts of our thought that come from ancient Rome and ancient Greece.

Poetry seems to have sprung from two sources.... First, the instinct of imitation is implanted in man from childhood...he is the most imitative of living creatures.... Next there is the instinct for harmony and rhythm, meter being manifestly sections of rhythm.

Aristotle, *The Poetics*

Some Elements of Poetry

Rhyme: the repetition of sound
- **End rhyme**: rhyme at the ends of lines of poetry
- **Internal rhyme**: rhymes inside the lines
- **Eye rhyme**: rhymes that look alike but do not sound alike
- **Rhyme scheme**: using letters to show the arrangement of rhyme
- **Onomatopoeia**: a word that sounds like what it describes
- **Alliteration**: the repetition of initial vowels or consonants

Meter: the pattern of rhythm of syllables
- **Stress**: the emphasis given to certain syllables in words
- **Foot**: the repeating unit of meter
- **Iamb**: a two-syllable foot with the stress on the second syllable
- **Trochee**: a two-syllable foot with the stress on the first syllable
- **Anapest**: a three-syllable foot with the stress on the third
- **Dactyl**: a three-syllable foot with the stress on the first
- **Iambic pentameter**: five iambs to a line of ten syllables

Stanza: a part of a poem, based on form of meter and rhyme
- **Quatrain**: a four-line stanza
- **Ballad**: a quatrain alternating iambic tetrameter and iambic trimeter. The rhyme scheme of a ballad is *abcb*.
- **English Sonnet**: a fourteen-line poem of four stanzas: three quatrains and a couplet. The rhyme scheme is *abab cdcd efef gg*.

Figures of Speech: comparisons that are not literally true

Simile: an openly expressed comparison using *like* or *as*

Metaphor: an implied comparison

Personification: Portraying an object as a person

Aristotle: a Greek philosopher who discussed poetry in 350 B.C.E. Aristotle was a student of Plato, who was a student of Socrates.

Questions for Review

1. The words *bargain* and *slain* are an example of:
   a. end rhyme
   b. eye rhyme
   c. internal rhyme
   d. alliteration

2. The words *boom* and *splat* are examples of:
   a. end rhyme
   b. eye rhyme
   c. alliteration
   d. onomatopoeia

3. When we begin words with the same sound, like *dark*, *dungeon*, *damp*, and *dew*, that is:
   a. eye rhyme
   b. alliteration
   c. onomatopoeia
   d. end rhyme

4. A line of iambic tetrameter has:
   a. one foot
   b. two feet
   c. three feet
   d. four feet

5. An iamb contains:
   a. one syllable
   b. two syllables
   c. three syllables
   d. four syllables

6. The word *balloon* is an example of a(n):

a. iamb
b. dactyl
c. trochee
d. anapest

7. The rhyme scheme of a ballad is:

a. *abcd*
b. *abcb*
c. *abab*
d. *abcc*

8. A ballad stanza contains:

a. one line
b. two lines
c. three lines
d. four lines

9. A ballad has iambic tetrameter in lines:

a. two and four
b. one and three
c. three and five
d. three and four

10. The words "O my Luve's like a red, red rose" contain a(n):

a. metaphor
b. eye rhyme
c. simile
d. onomatopoeia

11. The words "The truth is a stone at the bottom of the sea" contain a:
a. metaphor
b. ballad
c. simile
d. sonnet

12. A sonnet contains a couplet and:
a. one quatrain
b. two quatrains
c. three quatrains
d. four quatrains

13. A sonnet is written in:
a. iambic pentameter
b. trochaic tetrameter
c. dactylic trimeter
d. anapestic dimeter

14. The natural meter of the English language is:
a. iambic
b. trochaic
c. dactylic
d. anapestic

15. Shakespeare's line "Double, double, toil and trouble" is an example of:
a. iambic tetrameter
b. dactylic trimeter
c. trochaic tetrameter
d. anapestic pentameter

16. A pattern of lines that forms a section of a poem is called a(n):

a. meter
b. couplet
c. alliteration
d. stanza

17. The rhyme scheme *abab cdcd efef gg* is the scheme of a:

a. ballad
b. couplet
c. sonnet
d. quatrain

18. The name of Alexander the Great's teacher who wrote *The Poetics* was:

a. Aristotle
b. John Keats
c. Robert Burns
d. William Butler Yeats

19. A two-line stanza is called a:

a. dimeter
b. paradox
c. couplet
d. doublet

20. What poet said that the brain is wider than the sky?

a. William Butler Yeats
b. William Shakespeare
c. John Keats
d. Emily Dickinson

My heart is like a singing bird
Whose nest is in a watered shoot;
My heart is like an apple tree
Whose boughs are bent with thickset fruit;
My heart is like a rainbow shell
That paddles in a halcyon sea;
My heart is gladder than all these
Because my love is come to me.
– Christina Rossetti